I0822233

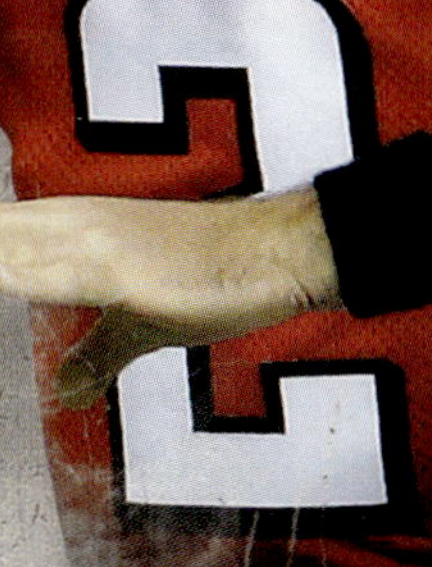

BY PHIL ERVIN

SportsZone
An Imprint of Abdo Publishing
abdopublishing.com

abdopublishing.com

Published by Abdo Publishing, a division of ABDO, PO Box 398166, Minneapolis, Minnesota 55439. Copyright © 2017 by Abdo Consulting Group, Inc. International copyrights reserved in all countries. No part of this book may be reproduced in any form without written permission from the publisher. SportsZone™ is a trademark and logo of Abdo Publishing.

Printed in the United States of America, North Mankato, Minnesota
042016
092016

Cover Photo: David Goldman/AP Images
Interior Photos: David Goldman/AP Images, 1; John Bazemore/AP Images, 4-5, 18-19, 28-29; Allen Kee/AP Images, 6, 20; Alan Mothner/AP Images, 7; Matthew Stockman/Allsport/Getty Images, 8-9; AP Images, 10-11, 14-15; Vernon Biever/AP Images, 12-13; Al Messerschmidt/AP Images, 16-17; Elise Amendola/AP Images, 21; Paul Abell/AP Images, 22-23; Darren Hauck/AP Images, 24-25; Chuck Burton/AP Images, 26; Kent Smith/AP Images, 27

Editor: Patrick Donnelly
Series Designer: Nikki Farinella

Cataloging-in-Publication Data
Names: Ervin, Phil, author.
Title: Atlanta Falcons / by Phil Ervin.
Description: Minneapolis, MN : Abdo Publishing, [2017] | Series: NFL up close | Includes index.
Identifiers: LCCN 2015960324 | ISBN 9781680782073 (lib. bdg.) | ISBN 9781680776188 (ebook)
Subjects: LCSH: Atlanta Falcons (Football team)--History--Juvenile literature. | National Football League--Juvenile literature. | Football--Juvenile literature. | Professional sports--Juvenile literature. | Football teams--Georgia--Juvenile literature.
Classification: DDC 796.332--dc23
LC record available at http://lccn.loc.gov/2015960324

TABLE OF CONTENTS

DIRTY BIRDS

In 1998, the Atlanta Falcons had a season to remember, both on and off the field. They took the National Football League (NFL) by storm with a 14-2 record and a crazy end zone dance that their fans loved to mimic.

The "Dirty Bird" dance became a popular sight in Atlanta that year. Running back Jamal Anderson is said to have invented it. Tight end O. J. Santiago helped popularize it when he started doing it in games, too. Players flapped their elbows like wings and jumped around after scoring touchdowns. They had plenty of chances to dance that year.

Jamal Anderson surges into the end zone against the San Francisco 49ers in a January 1999 playoff game.

Quarterback Chris Chandler had the best season of his 17-year career. Anderson rushed for 1,846 yards. Wide receivers Tony Martin and Terance Mathis both topped 1,000 receiving yards. And linebacker Jessie Tuggle led a strong defense.

But despite that great season, one team was even better that year. The Minnesota Vikings went 15-1 and set an NFL record for points scored. They chewed up their opponents all year. And they were waiting for the Falcons in Minneapolis. To get to the Super Bowl, the Falcons would have to beat the Vikings in the noisy Metrodome.

Atlanta quarterback Chris Chandler had a career year for the Falcons in 1998.

FAST FACT

Through 2015, Jamal Anderson's 1998 totals of 410 carries and 1,846 yards were still Falcons team records.

Falcons tight end O. J. Santiago demonstrates the "Dirty Bird."

The Falcons' defense kept the game close. Chandler led a drive to tie the game in the last minute on a touchdown pass to Mathis. In overtime, Morten Andersen made a 38-yard field goal to win the game. The Falcons did the "Dirty Bird" all over the field as the shocked Vikings fans filed out in silence. Even coach Dan Reeves did a version of the dance for the first time all year.

The Falcons went on to lose to the Denver Broncos in the Super Bowl. But the 1998 Falcons had left their footprints on the NFL.

Jamal Anderson and coach Dan Reeves do the "Dirty Bird" after clinching a trip to the Super Bowl in January 1999.

FAST FACT

The good times did not last long for the Falcons. They lost Jamal Anderson to a knee injury early in the 1999 season and slumped to a 5-11 record.

NFL Commissioner Pete Rozelle, *left*, presents an official certificate of membership to Falcons owner Rankin Smith on February 15, 1966.

FAST FACT
The Falcons' first helmets featured gold, black, and white stripes to represent rival universities Georgia and Georgia Tech.

SUNDAYS DOWN SOUTH

People all around the United States watch and play football. In the South, it is practically a religion. Many great players have come from the Atlanta area. High school and college football have a rich tradition throughout Georgia.

Pro football was another story. For years, the NFL did not have a team south of Washington, DC. But in 1966, the league added an expansion team in Atlanta. Local businessman Rankin Smith was the Falcons' first owner. A local radio station sponsored a contest to name the team. A high school teacher submitted the winning choice.

Tommy Nobis, *right*, was the first Atlanta player to have his jersey retired.

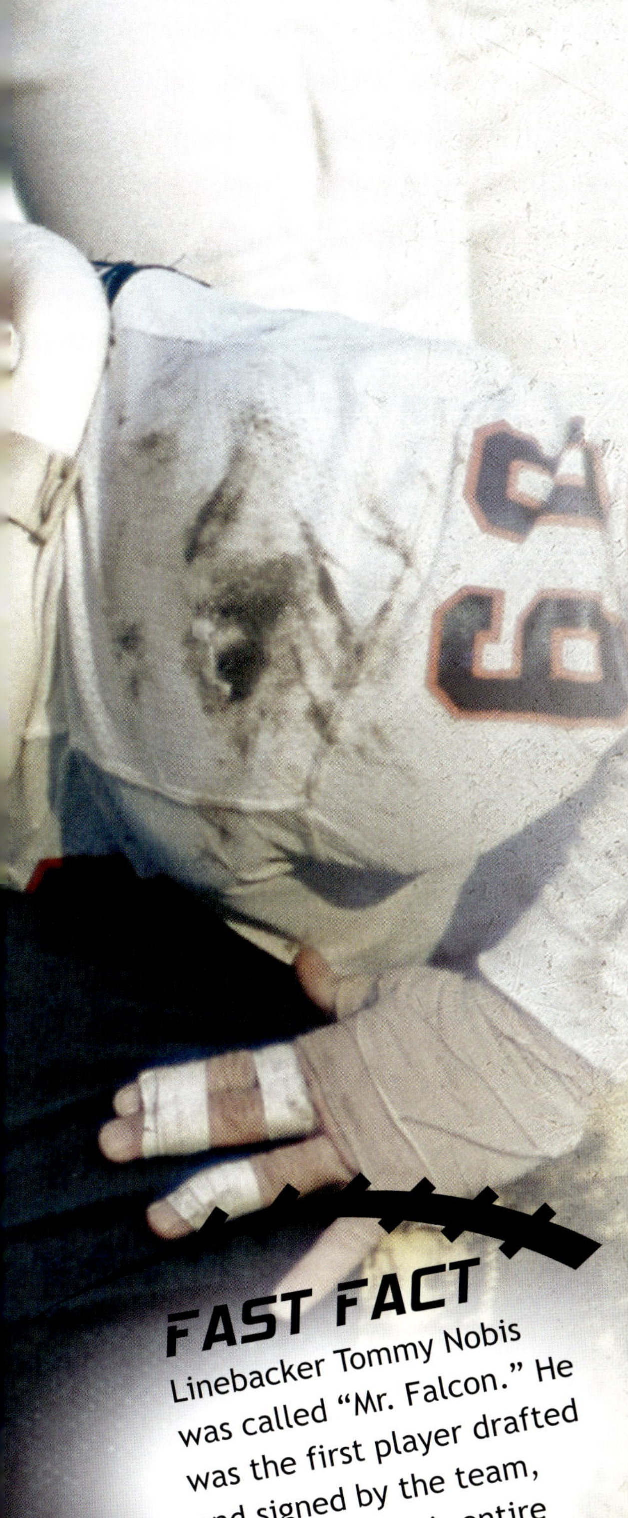

The Falcons' first coach was Norb Hecker, a longtime assistant under Green Bay Packers legend Vince Lombardi. But he did not last long. The Falcons won only four games in their first two seasons. Next up was former Minnesota Vikings coach Norm Van Brocklin. He had a bit more success. From 1971 to 1973, the Falcons went 23-18-1 and did not have a losing season.

But it would take a few more years—and a few more coaches—before the Falcons left their mark on the playoffs.

FAST FACT

Linebacker Tommy Nobis was called "Mr. Falcon." He was the first player drafted and signed by the team, and he played his entire 11-year career in Atlanta.

FALCONS TAKE FLIGHT

The Falcons selected quarterback Steve Bartkowski with the first overall pick of the 1975 NFL Draft. He fought through numerous injuries that caused him to miss games early in his career. But from his first day with the Falcons, Bartkowski was the team's starting quarterback.

Over the next 11 years, Bartkowski led the Falcons to the playoffs three times. In 1978, they qualified as a wild card. They hosted the Philadelphia Eagles in the first playoff game in team history. They were losing 13-0 in the fourth quarter, but Bartkowski threw two touchdown passes and the Falcons won 14-13.

FAST FACT

In 1992, the Falcons left their original home, Atlanta-Fulton County Stadium, and moved indoors to the Georgia Dome.

Steve Bartkowski led the Falcons past the Philadelphia Eagles in the 1978 playoffs.

In the next 15 years, some great players put on the Falcons uniform. Defensive end Claude Humphrey ended up in the Pro Football Hall of Fame. Running back William Andrews and center Jeff Van Note both had their numbers retired by the team.

Cornerback and kick returner Deion Sanders was one of the most electrifying NFL players ever. The Falcons drafted Sanders fifth overall in 1989. In five years with the team, he intercepted 24 passes and returned five kicks for touchdowns. One of his interceptions helped seal Atlanta's second playoff victory, a 27-20 win over the Saints in New Orleans in 1991.

FAST FACT

Deion Sanders also played Major League Baseball for four teams over nine years. He led the National League in triples in 1992.

Deion Sanders scores on a 68-yard punt return in his first NFL game on September 10, 1989, against the Los Angeles Rams.

FAST FACT

Dan Reeves coached the Falcons for seven seasons. His teams had a 49-59-1 record.

Dan Reeves gives a thumbs-up to the crowd after the Falcons beat the San Francisco 49ers in January 1999.

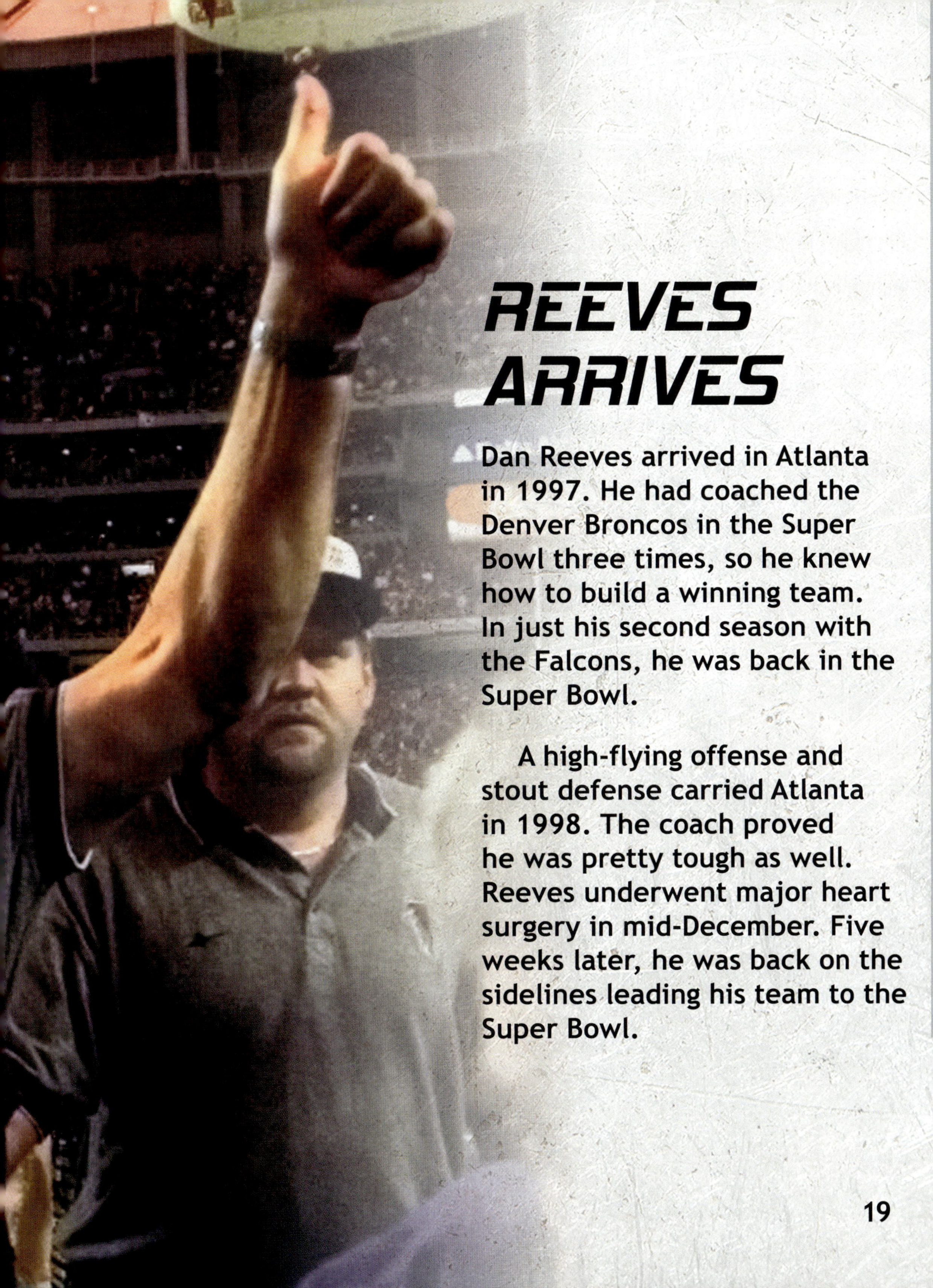

REEVES ARRIVES

Dan Reeves arrived in Atlanta in 1997. He had coached the Denver Broncos in the Super Bowl three times, so he knew how to build a winning team. In just his second season with the Falcons, he was back in the Super Bowl.

A high-flying offense and stout defense carried Atlanta in 1998. The coach proved he was pretty tough as well. Reeves underwent major heart surgery in mid-December. Five weeks later, he was back on the sidelines leading his team to the Super Bowl.

In the Super Bowl, Reeves faced his former team and many of his former players. The Broncos were still led by quarterback John Elway, who was playing in his final NFL game. He and Reeves had feuded at times in Denver. Beating the Broncos and Elway would make it that much sweeter for the Falcons and their coach.

But it was not to be. The Falcons took a 3-0 lead. Then Denver scored 31 of the next 34 points. Elway threw an 80-yard touchdown pass. Atlanta quarterback Chris Chandler was intercepted three times. The Broncos won 34-19.

Tim Dwight's kickoff return for a touchdown was one of the few Falcons highlights from the Super Bowl against Denver.

FAST FACT
Chris Chandler, Atlanta's quarterback in 1998, played for seven teams in his 17-year NFL career.

Chris Chandler shows his frustration during the Falcons' Super Bowl loss against the Broncos.

NEW WINGS

The Super Bowl buzz did not last long in Atlanta. By 2000, the Falcons were 4-12 and in last place in their division. They selected quarterback Michael Vick with the first pick in the 2001 draft. He became the starter by the end of the year.

Vick was a talented athlete. He had a cannon for an arm and was one of the fastest players in the league. He could beat opponents through the air or on the ground. He got the Falcons to the playoffs in 2002, and they won a playoff game on the road against the Green Bay Packers. Two years later, they were a game away from the Super Bowl but lost to the Philadelphia Eagles.

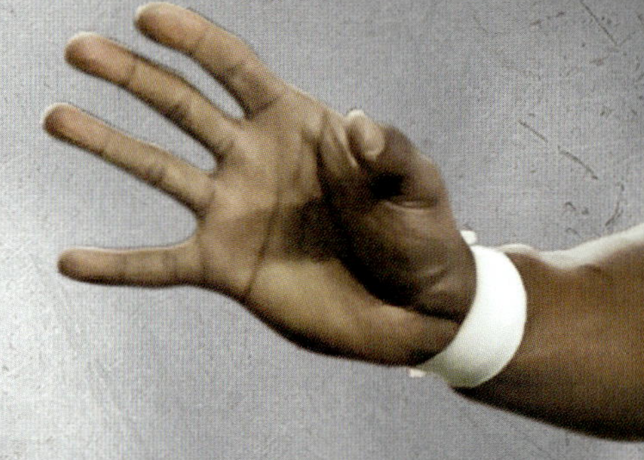

Michael Vick was known more for his running, but he was a dangerous passer as well.

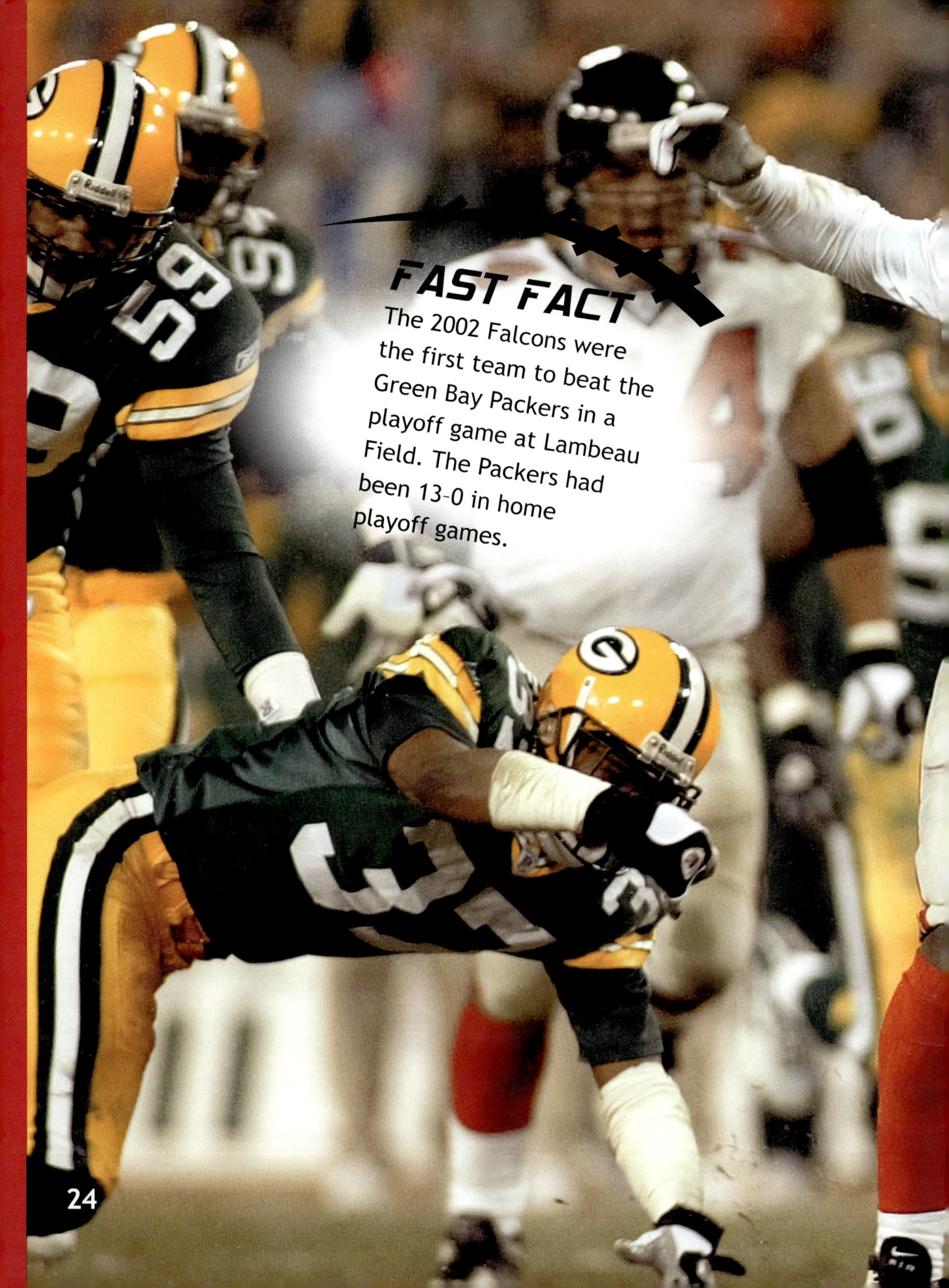

FAST FACT

The 2002 Falcons were the first team to beat the Green Bay Packers in a playoff game at Lambeau Field. The Packers had been 13-0 in home playoff games.

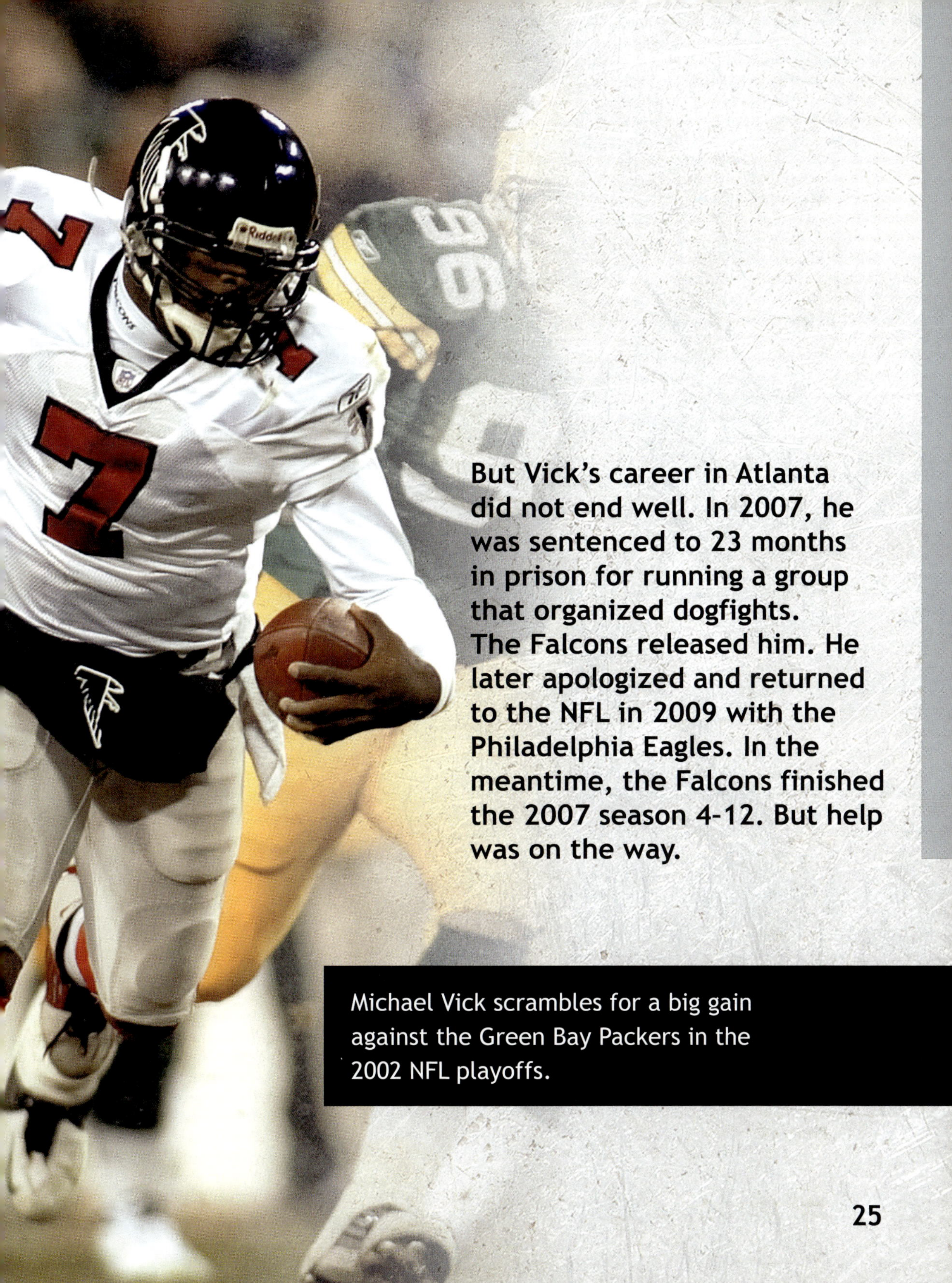

But Vick's career in Atlanta did not end well. In 2007, he was sentenced to 23 months in prison for running a group that organized dogfights. The Falcons released him. He later apologized and returned to the NFL in 2009 with the Philadelphia Eagles. In the meantime, the Falcons finished the 2007 season 4-12. But help was on the way.

Michael Vick scrambles for a big gain against the Green Bay Packers in the 2002 NFL playoffs.

ON THE VERGE

The Falcons used the third pick in the 2008 NFL Draft to bring in their next franchise quarterback. Matt Ryan immediately took over as the starter, and he clicked right away with wide receiver Roddy White. Running back Michael Turner rushed for 1,699 yards and 17 touchdowns that year. Together, they led the Falcons to the playoffs with an 11-5 record in 2008.

The Falcons had a winning record in each of Ryan's first five seasons. In 2012, they were back in the conference championship game, but they lost a thriller to the San Francisco 49ers.

Matt Ryan fires a pass during his rookie season.

Julio Jones, *right*, outleaps Panthers linebacker Luke Kuechly to make an amazing catch in a 2015 game.

The Falcons made another coaching change in 2015. Their defense had slipped to the bottom of the league rankings. They gave up more yards than any team in the league in 2014.

So they turned to Dan Quinn, the former defensive coordinator of the Seattle Seahawks. Quinn built some hard-hitting defenses in Seattle. In his first year with the Falcons, Quinn helped move their defensive ranking from 32nd—or dead last—to 16th in the league.

Pro Bowl cornerback Desmond Trufant, *21*, returns a fumble for a touchdown against the Houston Texans in 2015.

FAST FACT

Falcons wide receiver Julio Jones led the NFL with 136 catches and 1,871 receiving yards in 2015. Both totals were the second-highest in NFL history.

TIMELINE

1966
The Atlanta Falcons play their first season in the NFL.

1978
On Christmas Eve, the Falcons play their first-ever playoff game, beating the Philadelphia Eagles 14-13.

1980
The Falcons go 12-4 and win their first division title.

1997
Dan Reeves takes over as the 11th coach in Falcons history.

1999
On January 17, Morten Andersen's 38-yard field goal in overtime lifts the Falcons past the Minnesota Vikings for their first Super Bowl berth. They go on to lose to the Denver Broncos 34-19.

2001
Atlanta drafts quarterback Michael Vick first overall. He flourishes in Atlanta until he is sent to prison in 2007 and cut by the Falcons.

2008
The Falcons draft quarterback Matt Ryan with the third overall pick. He leads the team to the playoffs as a rookie.

2013
On January 20, the Falcons fall one game short of the Super Bowl, losing to the San Francisco 49ers 28-24.

GLOSSARY

BERTH
A place, listing, or role.

COORDINATOR
An assistant coach who is in charge of the offense or defense.

EXPANSION
When a league grows by adding new teams.

FEUD
Argument or disagreement.

FRANCHISE QUARTERBACK
A quarterback who leads a team for a number of years.

INTERCEPTION
When a defensive player catches a pass intended for an offensive player.

MIMIC
Imitate.

RETRACTABLE
Able to be opened and closed.

WILD CARD
A team that makes the playoffs even though it did not win its division.

INDEX

ABOUT THE AUTHOR

Phil Ervin was born and raised in Omaha, Nebraska. He has covered sports for Fox Sports and newspapers in Missouri and Georgia. He is a graduate of Benedictine College in Atchison, Kansas.